Stephanie Olds

Role Diffusion: Why Capable People Leave Work They're Good At

Role Diffusion: Why Capable People Leave Work They're Good At by Stephanie Olds

Printed in the United States of America January 2026

ISBN 978-1968178352

Ink and Revival Publishing Virginia, USA

Table of Contents

A Note

This book is offered in recognition of those whose
competence was relied upon,
whose concerns were deferred,
and whose clarity was earned through resistance rather than
support.

Stephanie Olds

STATEMENT OF INQUIRY

This book was written because a pattern kept repeating itself in ways that existing language could not adequately explain. In role after role, across teams, organizations, and industries, capable people were taking on work they were good at, work they often enjoyed, and work that clearly mattered, only to find themselves stalled, contained, or quietly pushed toward exit once the weight of that work outgrew the roles meant to hold it. The explanations offered for these outcomes rarely matched the experience of the people living inside them. Burnout was named where exhaustion had not yet arrived. Boundary-setting was prescribed where no clear boundary had ever been drawn. Ambition was questioned where the real issue was misalignment between responsibility and recognition. The gap between what people were doing and how their work was formally understood widened, and yet there was no shared language to describe that widening without personalizing it as failure.

The absence of language matters because systems rely on what can be named and managed. When a phenomenon cannot be clearly described, it is easily dismissed, normalized, or reframed as an individual problem rather than a structural one. With continued exposure, I began to recognize that what people were responding to was not simply workload or pace, but the quiet migration of responsibility away from formal roles and into individuals who were able and willing to absorb it. This migration did not require approval, documentation, or redesign. It happened through trust, convenience, and necessity, and once it occurred, it was rarely reversed. The people carrying that responsibility often could not point to a single moment when it was assigned, which made it difficult to challenge without sounding resistant or uncooperative.

The term Role Diffusion emerged as a way to name this pattern with precision rather than accusation. It describes a condition in which responsibility expands informally while authority, compensation, and role clarity remain formally fixed, allowing systems to stabilize around individual competence instead of structural design. This framing matters because it relocates the source of the imbalance. Rather than asking why individuals failed to cope, advocate, or endure, it asks how systems learned to depend on informal labor without formally acknowledging it. The shift from personal explanation to structural mechanism is not semantic; it changes how the experience is understood and what kinds of responses become possible.

This work is grounded in observation rather than institutional research protocols, shaped by years of applied leadership and systems work rather than academic appointment. The methodology is qualitative, experiential, and pattern-based, drawing from repeated encounters with the same mechanism operating under different names and justifications. The goal is not to claim universality, but to offer a framework that explains a recurring organizational dynamic more accurately than existing terms have done. Where possible, the book distinguishes Role Diffusion from adjacent concepts not to compete with them, but to clarify where they fall short of explaining why capable people so often leave work they are good at despite continued performance and commitment.

The perspective offered here is that of a practitioner-scholar, someone situated inside the systems being described rather than observing them from a distance. That position carries both insight and limitation. It allows for close attention to how responsibility actually moves through organizations, how ambiguity is operationalized, and how formal structures respond when informal arrangements begin to strain. It also means that the analysis privileges lived mechanics over controlled measurement. This book does not attempt to quantify Role Diffusion across populations, nor does it propose a single corrective model that can be universally applied. Its contribution lies instead in naming, describing, and tracing a mechanism that has remained largely invisible despite its consequences.

A single composite case appears throughout the book, not as autobiography and not as evidence of harm, but as a way to illustrate how Role Diffusion progresses when informal labor collides with formal systems. That case is deliberately anonymized and depersonalized, used to demonstrate structural response rather than personal impact. The intent is not to adjudicate outcomes or argue intent, but to show how systems behave when confronted with the limits of their own design. Formal escalation, including legal or grievance processes, is treated here not as the focal point of the story, but as an inevitable juncture that arises when informal responsibility has nowhere else to go.

This book does not seek to replace institutional scholarship, nor does it claim the authority of credentialed research. It occupies a different, older tradition of theory formation, one rooted in careful observation, clear language, and the willingness to name what has been operating without a name. Its success is not measured by formal validation, but by whether readers recognize the pattern earlier than they otherwise would have, and whether that recognition allows for more honest decisions about work, responsibility, and departure. If Role Diffusion becomes a term others use, challenge, refine, or reject, it will have served its purpose by making the invisible visible.

What follows is an attempt to walk carefully through this concept, neither sensationalizing it nor minimizing its effects. The aim is clarity without drama, rigor without gatekeeping, and language that holds both individuals and systems accountable to the truth of how work is actually carried. Role Diffusion is not presented here as a moral failure or a crisis narrative, but as a design problem that has been quietly shaping careers and organizations alike. Naming it does not resolve it, but it creates the conditions under which resolution becomes possible, which is where any serious inquiry must begin.

INTRODUCTION

The Quiet Break

How work fractures long before anyone calls it a problem

———————◆❖◆———————

There are people who leave work they are good at not because the work is hard, but because something in the relationship between effort and reward quietly breaks. It does not happen all at once. There is no single meeting, no dramatic confrontation, no obvious turning point others can point to later and say, *That's when it went wrong.* Instead, it unfolds slowly, in a way that is easy to explain away while it is happening and difficult to articulate once it has passed. The person is capable, dependable, often well-liked. The work matters to them. They stay longer than most would. And when they finally leave, the reaction around them is almost always the same: surprise.

That surprise exists because what drove the departure was never visible in a clean or formal way. On paper, the role still looked reasonable. The title had not changed. The job description still fit inside a familiar box. Yet the lived experience of the work no longer matched what the role claimed to be, and the gap between the two widened quietly until the person standing in it could no longer pretend it was manageable. What they were carrying had grown heavier, but not in a way that could be measured easily or named without sounding ungrateful. They were not drowning in tasks so much as absorbing responsibility that never seemed to belong to anyone else, and that distinction matters because responsibility carries weight even when it does not come with authority.

It often begins with something small and reasonable, the kind of request that sounds like trust rather than transfer. Can you help with this? Can you cover that for now? Can you take a look, just until we figure it out? The person says yes because they can, because it feels aligned with their values, because they believe competence will eventually be met with clarity. Little by little, those yeses start to stack, not dramatically but persistently, until the role expands in directions that were never formally discussed. Nothing has been taken away from them; things have only been added. The absence of subtraction is what makes the expansion hard to see, and harder still to challenge.

As the work grows, so does reliance. Questions begin routing toward the same person. Decisions default to them without being officially assigned. When problems arise, their name surfaces first, not because they hold authority, but because they have history, context, and an internal sense of ownership that others have not been asked to develop. This reliance is often framed as appreciation. You're the one we trust. You always get it done. We couldn't do this without you. The words feel affirming at first, until it becomes clear that trust is being offered in place of structure, and appreciation in place of recognition that carries material weight.

At some point, the person notices that while their responsibility has grown, their position has not. Colleagues advance into new roles. Titles shift. Opportunities circulate. The explanation, when it comes, is usually delivered gently, as if it were a compliment. You're too important where you are. We need you right now. This role would fall apart without you. What is being said is not unkind, but it carries a quiet finality. Advancement is framed as disruption. Stability is preserved by keeping the same person in the same place, even as the work they do no longer resembles the role they hold.

This is the moment when fairness, not fatigue, begins to erode trust. The person does not feel incapable. They feel misaligned. They can see the work clearly enough to know it exceeds what is being acknowledged, yet not clearly enough to point to a single clause or policy that captures the difference. When they try to name it, they are met with familiar language. Other duties as assigned. Flexible roles. Everyone pitches in. The language is not false, but it is incomplete, and its incompleteness is doing real work for the system by keeping the expansion informal and therefore unaccountable.

Eventually, the person looks for a formal way to reconcile what they are doing with how they are positioned. They ask for reclassification, adjustment, relief, or recognition that matches the reality of the work. When those conversations fail to move anything structurally, they are left with fewer options than it appears from the outside. There is no informal path left to try. The only remaining avenue is a formal one, not because the person wants conflict, but because the gap between lived labor and written role has become impossible to hold privately. When they turn to a formal process, whether through HR, grievance channels, or legal structures, it is often described later as escalation, as though something has been made bigger than it needed to be, rather than as what happens when informal systems refuse to correct themselves.

In one such case, a capable employee in a large organization found themselves in this position after years of absorbing work well beyond their formal scope. They had stayed because they believed the system would eventually align effort with recognition, and because they cared about the outcomes they were responsible for, even when those outcomes were not officially theirs to own. When they sought a formal remedy, the response they encountered focused narrowly on job descriptions and classifications, as though the lived reality of the work could be reduced to what had been written long before it evolved. The process did not meaningfully resolve the imbalance. The organization stabilized. The role remained unchanged. The employee eventually left, carrying with them not a sense of failure, but a lingering question about why staying had required so much personal accommodation.

What is striking about cases like this is not that they happen, but that they happen so often under different names. In government, it appears as reliance without reclassification. In healthcare, as care work absorbed without relief. In education, as emotional and administrative labor quietly layered onto teaching. In nonprofits, as mission standing in for structure. In tech, as ownership expanding faster than authority. The surface conditions differ, but the mechanism is the same. Responsibility migrates informally. Authority remains fixed. Ambiguity is preserved because it benefits continuity. And the person at the center is left to manage the cost of that imbalance until they cannot.

This book names that mechanism as Role Diffusion, not to assign blame, but to restore clarity where confusion has been allowed to linger. It is not a book about burnout, though burnout may follow. It is not a book about boundaries, though boundaries are often recommended too late. It is about what happens when systems reward competence with expansion but withhold the structural changes that would make that expansion honest. It is about why good people leave work they are good at, not because they lack resilience, but because they recognize when a role no longer tells the truth about the work it requires.

Naming something does not undo what has already happened, but it does something equally important. It gives people language before the damage becomes personal, before fairness erodes into resentment, before leaving feels like the only remaining form of self-respect. Role Diffusion thrives in silence and ambiguity. It weakens when it is made visible. What follows is an effort to make it visible, not all at once, but carefully, so that the reader can recognize it as it unfolds and decide, with clarity rather than shame, what they are willing to carry and what they are not.

Part I

The Invisible Expansion

Most people do not leave work because it is difficult. They leave because something inside the work stops making sense. The hours may be long, the expectations demanding, and the pace unrelenting, yet none of those conditions alone explain why capable, committed people eventually disengage from roles they once handled with confidence. What precedes departure is often quieter than burnout and harder to name than dissatisfaction. It begins as a feeling that responsibility has shifted without being acknowledged, and that what is being asked no longer matches what is being recognized.

Part I begins in this quiet space, where expansion is gradual and rarely contested. Responsibilities accumulate because someone notices what needs doing and steps in. Decisions widen because someone has the judgment to make them. Risk migrates because someone can see consequences before they occur. None of this feels wrong at first. In fact, it often feels like growth. The system rewards reliability, trusts competence, and leans on those who do not let things fall apart. Over time, however, the role itself remains unchanged, even as the work it contains becomes something else entirely.

This section traces how that shift happens without ceremony. It shows how informal responsibility becomes normalized, how clarity erodes while performance remains strong, and how individuals begin carrying work that exists outside the boundaries of their titles. The problem here is not that people are doing too much. It is that the work is no longer being named accurately, and unnamed work has a way of disappearing into expectation.

Part I is not about failure or mismanagement. It is about how systems quietly adapt around capability, allowing roles to stretch without ever being redesigned. By the time discomfort surfaces, the expansion has already been absorbed, and the person inside the role has often been praised for the very flexibility that now limits them. This is where Role Diffusion takes root, not through conflict or collapse, but through success carried too far without structural truth.

CHAPTER 1

What Role Diffusion Is (and Is Not)

How responsibility migrates without being acknowledged

Role Diffusion is easiest to misunderstand because it rarely announces itself as a problem. It does not arrive with conflict or complaint, and it does not begin in opposition to the organization or the work. It begins inside competence. It takes root when someone is good at what they do, trusted to handle complexity, and willing to step in where gaps exist. That willingness is not a flaw. It is often the very quality that made the role feel meaningful in the first place, which is why the early stages of Role Diffusion feel less like exploitation and more like contribution.

Because it starts there, Role Diffusion is often mistaken for growth. More responsibility is equated with advancement, even when no formal change accompanies it. The work expands, the expectations deepen, and the outcomes matter more, yet the role itself remains unchanged. On paper, everything looks stable. In practice, the person is now carrying responsibilities that shape outcomes without holding the authority to shape decisions. This distinction is subtle enough to be overlooked, yet powerful enough to alter the entire relationship between the individual and the system they work within. However, what remains invisible in that stability is the growing distance between responsibility and authority, a distance that cannot be reconciled simply by continuing to perform well.

What defines Role Diffusion is not simply having a lot to do. It is the quiet migration of responsibility away from formal structures and toward an individual, without a corresponding migration of authority, compensation, or role clarity. The work does not just increase in volume; it increases in consequence. Decisions made elsewhere land on the individual's shoulders to execute, fix, explain, or absorb. In cumulative sequence, they become accountable for outcomes they cannot fully influence, and that misalignment begins to distort how success and failure are experienced.

This is where Role Diffusion diverges from burnout, though the two are often conflated. Burnout describes a state of depletion, a point at which energy, motivation, or capacity has been exhausted. Role Diffusion describes a condition that exists long before depletion sets in. Many people experiencing Role Diffusion are not burned out at all. They are still capable, still engaged, still producing high-quality work. What troubles them is not that they cannot continue, but that continuing requires them to quietly accept an arrangement that no longer feels fair or truthful. Therefore, treating Role Diffusion as an issue of endurance rather than design delays recognition of the problem until depletion becomes unavoidable.

It is also not a matter of poor boundaries, despite how frequently that explanation is offered. Boundaries imply a clear line that has been crossed and could have been defended if only the individual had acted differently. Role Diffusion operates precisely because the line is never drawn in a clear or formal way. The expansion happens incrementally, through reasonable requests and situational needs, each one defensible on its own. By the time the person realizes the role has changed, the change has already been normalized, and pulling back feels less like boundary-setting and more like withdrawal from responsibilities the system now depends on.

Nor is Role Diffusion the same as scope creep, which tends to be project-based and time-bound, visible enough to be documented and corrected. Role Diffusion is relational and ongoing. It reshapes how work flows through a system and who absorbs uncertainty when things are unclear. It persists precisely because it remains informal, protected by language that suggests flexibility while obscuring permanence. Other duties as assigned becomes not a footnote, but a foundation, allowing sustained expansion without the obligation to redesign the role honestly.

The danger in misnaming Role Diffusion lies in what misnaming allows systems to avoid. When the issue is framed as individual burnout, the solution becomes rest. When it is framed as a boundary issue, the solution becomes self-advocacy. When it is framed as ambition or impatience, the solution becomes waiting. Each of these responses locates responsibility for correction inside the individual, even though the imbalance was produced structurally. Role Diffusion, by contrast, relocates the source of the problem back to the system, where informal labor has been allowed to substitute for formal design.

Understanding what Role Diffusion is also requires clarity about what it is not accusing. It is not an allegation of malicious intent. Most instances of Role Diffusion arise not from cruelty, but from convenience, risk aversion, and the quiet incentives that reward continuity over correction. Systems learn quickly where competence resides and then organize themselves around it. Once that organization stabilizes, changing it becomes costly, and so the path of least resistance is to leave the structure untouched and rely on the individual to continue absorbing the excess. Yet intent alone does not neutralize impact.

For the person inside it, the experience often feels confusing not because it lacks logic, but because it contains two truths at once. They are valued, and they are contained. They are trusted, and they are stalled. They are relied upon, and they are replaceable in theory, though not in practice. Holding these contradictions across months and years creates a particular kind of strain, one rooted less in exhaustion than in misalignment between effort and acknowledgment. The work no longer reflects back an honest picture of the role, and the role no longer reflects back an honest picture of the work.

Role Diffusion names this condition without assigning fault or prescribing immediate action. It offers a lens rather than a verdict, allowing individuals to see the shape of what they are carrying and how it came to rest with them. By naming it, the experience shifts from something vaguely personal to something recognizably structural, and that shift matters because it restores agency without demanding self-blame. Before anyone can decide what to do about Role Diffusion, they have to be able to see it clearly, not as a failure of endurance or ambition, but as a predictable outcome of how systems manage competence under ambiguity. As a result, the strain that emerges is not emotional fragility but cognitive dissonance, produced by holding responsibility without the power to shape its conditions.

Seeing it clearly does not resolve it, but it changes the internal conversation. It moves the question from *Why can't I keep doing this?* to *Why is this work being held this way?* That question opens the door to understanding how Role Diffusion unfolds, how it becomes normalized, and why it so often leads capable people to leave work they are good at, not because they lacked commitment, but because the role itself stopped telling the truth.

CHAPTER 2

How Responsibility Migrates Without Permission

Why expansion feels productive before it feels wrong

―――――――――――――――――――――⋄⟨❖⟩⋄――――――――――――――――――――

Responsibility rarely moves all at once. It drifts. It shifts a little at a time, following paths of least resistance rather than formal channels, and because it does so quietly, it often goes unnoticed until it has already settled somewhere new. In workplaces where roles are loosely defined or stretched by necessity, responsibility tends to migrate toward the person who can hold it without immediate disruption. This is not because they asked for more, but because the system learned, through repetition, that giving it to them works.

That learning begins innocently enough. A question lands in the wrong inbox, and instead of redirecting it, the capable person answers it. A task falls between roles, and rather than letting it stall, they complete it. A meeting needs facilitation, a decision needs follow-through, a problem needs resolution, and the person who understands the context steps in because they can see the consequence of delay. Each action is reasonable. Each choice feels aligned with competence and professionalism. None of it feels like a transfer of ownership at the time.

What makes this migration possible is that responsibility does not require permission to be absorbed. Authority must be granted. Titles must be approved. Compensation must be justified. Responsibility, by contrast, can simply be taken on, especially when it arrives framed as temporary, situational, or collaborative. The system does not resist this absorption because it benefits from it. Problems get solved. Work continues. Gaps are covered. No redesign is required, and no one has to acknowledge that the role has begun to change. However, once responsibility is absorbed, it rarely returns to the structure from which it came.

Through steady repetition, patterns form. The same person is consulted again. The same name appears in emails that have nothing to do with their formal duties but everything to do with outcomes. When something goes wrong, eyes turn toward the person who knows the most, even if they were never assigned the authority to prevent the issue in the first place. Responsibility starts to follow familiarity rather than structure, and familiarity deepens as the person continues to respond.

This is where Role Diffusion becomes self-reinforcing. Each instance of stepping in strengthens the perception that this is where the responsibility belongs. What began as assistance slowly becomes expectation. The system stops asking whether the work should live there and instead assumes that it does. Because no explicit handoff ever occurred, there is no moment to contest the transfer. The responsibility simply arrives, already normalized, already attached to the person who has proven they will carry it.

The language surrounding this migration often obscures what is happening. Words like help, support, collaboration, and flexibility soften the reality of sustained responsibility transfer. They suggest shared effort even when accountability quietly consolidates in one place. The person absorbing the work may still be excluded from decision-making conversations, even as they are held accountable for execution. This separation allows the system to enjoy the benefits of distributed labor while maintaining centralized authority, a configuration that feels efficient until it becomes brittle. Therefore, what appears collaborative on the surface slowly consolidates accountability in practice.

What is rarely acknowledged is that responsibility carries risk, not just workload. When outcomes matter, someone is implicitly responsible for preventing failure, managing fallout, and absorbing consequences. As responsibility migrates without permission, that risk migrates as well, landing on individuals who did not consent to hold it in a formal sense. They may not be blamed openly, but they feel the weight of knowing that if something breaks, they will be the one expected to fix it, explain it, or quietly make it disappear.

Because this process unfolds incrementally, it is easy for the individual to believe they are still operating within the bounds of their role. The system reinforces this belief by continuing to reference the formal job description when questions of recognition or advancement arise. The contradiction between what the person does and what the role claims they do becomes increasingly difficult to reconcile, yet pointing it out feels risky because the migration was never officially sanctioned. To challenge it is to disrupt something that now appears essential to the organization's functioning. As a result, individuals begin managing consequences they were never formally empowered to prevent.

This is why Role Diffusion is rarely corrected early. Correcting it would require the system to pause and ask uncomfortable questions about design, resourcing, and accountability. It would require acknowledging that responsibility has been allowed to travel farther than authority, and that someone has been quietly compensating for that imbalance. It is far easier to let the arrangement continue, especially when the person carrying the responsibility continues to perform well.

For the individual, the moment of recognition often comes not when the work feels overwhelming, but when it feels mis-owned. They realize they are making decisions in practice that they are not empowered to make in principle, or they are expected to manage outcomes without being included in the conversations that shape them. The work has followed them, but the role has not. That realization introduces a subtle shift in how the work feels, replacing pride with unease and commitment with calculation.

Responsibility that migrates without permission does not announce itself as unfair. It presents itself as necessary, reasonable, even flattering. Yet as the pattern matures, it reshapes the role into something that exists more in practice than on paper, leaving the person inside it to navigate contradictions that the system has no incentive to resolve. This is how Role Diffusion takes hold, not through force or intent, but through quiet accommodation, until the work being done and the role being held no longer describe the same reality, and the distance between them becomes impossible to ignore. In this way, Role Diffusion completes its quiet transfer, not through decision, but through accommodation.

CHAPTER 3

The Myth of "Other Duties as Assigned"

How flexibility becomes a shield for avoidance

———————————◆◆◆◆———————————

Most position descriptions contain a line that appears harmless enough, a phrase meant to acknowledge that no role can anticipate every situation or contingency. *"Other duties as assigned"* reads like flexibility, like realism, like an understanding that work is dynamic rather than fixed. In its original intent, the clause exists to cover incidental tasks, short-term needs, or occasional deviations that arise in the normal course of work. It is meant to serve the role, not redefine it, and to absorb the unexpected without requiring constant formal revision. However, when this clause becomes the primary justification for sustained expansion, it stops functioning as a footnote and begins operating as a mechanism.

That shift rarely happens abruptly. Instead, the clause is invoked casually at first, often in moments where the need feels legitimate and time-sensitive. Someone needs to step in. A gap has appeared. A process is unclear. Because the work matters and delay carries consequences, the capable person agrees, trusting that the flexibility implied by the clause is mutual and temporary. The system, however, reads the outcome rather than the intention. The task was completed. The problem was resolved. Therefore, the arrangement is treated as viable, even though no one has paused to ask whether it should be made permanent.

As responsibilities mount, the clause begins to function less as an exception and more as a rationale. Work that would normally require redesign, reclassification, or redistribution is absorbed instead by the same role, justified repeatedly under the same language. Because the clause already exists, its invocation feels procedurally sound, even as the substance of the role drifts farther from its original definition. What was meant to allow for flexibility now allows for avoidance, sparing the system from confronting the mismatch between what the role was designed to do and what it is now required to carry.

This is where the myth takes hold, because the clause creates the illusion that the work still belongs to the role as written. If the duties are "other," then they are assumed to be secondary, even when they have become central to outcomes. If they are "assigned," then someone is presumed to be accountable for the assignment itself, even when no formal decision was made. The language blurs responsibility in a way that protects structure while exposing individuals. Yet the clarity it offers is rhetorical rather than operational, and the longer it is relied upon, the less accurately the role describes reality.

Leaders often defend the use of this clause by appealing to practicality. Work has to get done. Budgets are constrained. Headcount is limited. Roles cannot be rewritten every time conditions change. All of this is true, and yet it is incomplete. Flexibility is not the same as permanence, and adaptability does not absolve systems of the responsibility to redesign roles when the nature of the work has materially shifted. When other duties as assigned becomes the standing explanation for outcome-critical labor, the role description becomes a fiction that no longer guides evaluation, advancement, or equity in any meaningful way.

What makes this particularly corrosive is that experienced leaders understand the difference between incidental tasks and sustained responsibility, even if they do not name it explicitly. They know when a role has grown beyond its original scope, and they know when the clause is being used to buy time rather than to reflect reality. However, acknowledging that growth would require action, and action carries cost. It may require admitting that the role was misdesigned, that reliance has outpaced structure, or that someone has been carrying more than was formally recognized. Therefore, the clause is allowed to stand in for resolution, even as the imbalance it conceals deepens.

For the individual inside the role, this creates a peculiar kind of paralysis. They are told that the work they are doing is part of their job, even as the job itself remains unchanged. When they ask for recognition, relief, or redesign, the response points back to the clause as evidence that the work was always included, even though it was never named, weighted, or valued as such. This circular logic makes it difficult to argue for change without sounding as though one is resisting the role itself, rather than questioning how honestly it reflects the work required.

In one composite case that will reappear throughout this book, this clause surfaced not as casual justification, but as formal defense. When the employee sought to demonstrate that their responsibilities had expanded into the functional territory of an entirely different role, the organization responded by pointing to the phrase *"other duties as assigned"* as though it were sufficient to absorb years of outcome-critical work. However, the reliance on that language did more than explain flexibility; it effectively erased the distinction between incidental tasks and sustained role substitution, allowing the system to argue continuity where redesign had been refused. What was presented as procedural consistency functioned instead as concealment, undercutting the possibility of fair evaluation by treating structural expansion as though it had always been part of the job.

In essence, the clause begins to function as a quiet silencer. It closes off conversation rather than opening it, because it frames expansion as compliance rather than evolution. The individual is left managing responsibilities that shape outcomes while lacking the authority or compensation that would normally accompany them, and yet the language used to justify this arrangement suggests there is nothing to discuss. Flexibility has hardened into expectation, and expectation has been normalized into design without ever being formally acknowledged.

This is one of the ways Role Diffusion sustains itself, because the clause provides cover for informal labor to become permanent without triggering structural review. It allows systems to benefit from adaptability while avoiding the work of alignment. In quiet progression, this avoidance erodes trust, not because the work is demanding, but because the language used to describe it no longer matches its reality. The role stops telling the truth, and the person inside it is asked to live with that discrepancy as though it were simply part of being professional.

Eventually, the tension created by this mismatch surfaces, not as complaint, but as a quiet recalibration of what the individual is willing to give. They may continue performing well, yet their relationship to the work changes as they recognize that flexibility has been interpreted as consent to indefinite expansion. When no honest conversation follows, the clause that once seemed benign becomes emblematic of a system unwilling to see the labor it relies on. And it is here, in the space between what is written and what is required, that Role Diffusion moves from inconvenience to inevitability, setting the stage for the dependency that follows.

CHAPTER 4

Why High Performers Are Most at Risk

Why competence attracts responsibility faster than relief

—◆◈◆—

High performers rarely enter roles expecting to be overextended or underrecognized. They arrive with a willingness to learn, a capacity to handle complexity, and an instinct to take responsibility seriously, which is often what earns them trust early on. That trust becomes the foundation upon which Role Diffusion builds, because systems are not neutral in how they distribute uncertainty. They move it toward those who can absorb it without immediate failure, and high performers, by definition, are capable of doing exactly that.

This capability creates a subtle but consequential asymmetry. While others are protected by the boundaries of their roles, high performers are granted access beyond those boundaries, often framed as opportunity rather than exposure. They are asked to weigh in, to step in, to see further than their title requires, and because they can see the implications of inaction, they respond. However, the same qualities that make their contributions valuable also make their labor easier to extract informally, especially when no immediate disruption follows.

As seasons change, competence begins to function as a signal rather than a trait. It signals availability, elasticity, and tolerance for ambiguity. The system learns that when complexity arises, it can route it toward the same individual and expect resolution without formal adjustment. Therefore, responsibility accumulates not because the person seeks it, but because the system recognizes where it will land safely. Authority, meanwhile, remains fixed, not out of malice, but because moving it would require acknowledging how much the role has already changed.

This is where high performance becomes a trap rather than a pathway. Advancement is typically framed as reward; however, for someone whose role has expanded informally, advancement represents disruption. Promoting them would expose the volume and significance of the work they have been carrying, forcing redistribution or redesign that the system has quietly avoided. As a result, high performers are often told they are indispensable, a statement that sounds affirming while simultaneously limiting their movement. They are held in place by their own effectiveness.

In the composite case threaded through this book, this dynamic became unmistakable when the individual sought to move into a new role after years of sustained overextension. Leadership delayed the transfer not because a successor had been identified, but because no one could immediately be named who was capable of fulfilling the responsibilities that had quietly accumulated. The delay was framed as logistical rather than structural, yet the implication was clear: the system could not release the individual without first solving a problem it had long refused to formally acknowledge.

What followed exposed the contradiction at the heart of Role Diffusion. The role remained vacant far longer than anticipated, not because the work had diminished, but because the level of responsibility required could not be easily absorbed by someone at the same classification. When the position was eventually filled, it was assigned to someone at a higher pay level, confirming what had already been evident in practice. The work had always been valued at that level; it had simply been carried, for a time, without compensation or redesign.

This sequence is not an anomaly. It reveals how systems behave when warned in advance about misalignment and choose delay over correction. High performers often articulate these risks clearly, explaining that the scope of responsibility has outgrown the role and that replacement will require either redistribution or elevation. Yet those warnings are frequently discounted as negotiation rather than diagnosis. The system continues to benefit from the existing arrangement while postponing the cost of change, even when the individual makes explicit that the work cannot be sustainably held at the current level.

When leadership refuses to adjust role or compensation despite clear evidence, the situation moves from misalignment into inevitability. The individual is left with few options: continue enabling a structure that relies on undercompensated labor, or withdraw from the arrangement altogether. At this point, legal or formal action is not escalation in the emotional sense, but a consequence of having exhausted every informal avenue for correction. The system has already decided that continuity matters more than fairness, and therefore any challenge to that decision must pass through formal channels.

High performers often internalize this progression longer than others would, partly because they still care about outcomes. They see the downstream effects of their departure or disengagement, and they hesitate to create disruption for teams, missions, or public responsibilities they value. This sense of stewardship deepens the system's dependence, because it delays rupture while increasing exposure. However, stewardship without authority eventually becomes self-erasing, as the individual realizes that their restraint is being used to justify inaction.

What distinguishes Role Diffusion among high performers is that dissatisfaction emerges not from lack of challenge, but from lack of truth. The work remains engaging, the problems remain solvable, and the individual remains capable. What shifts is the realization that excellence is being used to postpone structural honesty. The system praises performance while refusing to align role, pay, or authority with what is actually required, and that refusal communicates something more decisive than any compliment.

Because high performers continue to perform well, their concerns are often reframed as impatience, ambition, or misinterpretation. The system reads ongoing success as evidence that the arrangement is viable, even as it quietly prepares for the disruption it claims to be avoiding. Therefore, when departure finally occurs, it is framed as unexpected, despite the fact that it followed repeated warnings and prolonged delay. What the system loses in that moment is not simply a capable employee, but the opportunity to correct itself before correction became unavoidable.

In this way, high performers are not merely more likely to experience Role Diffusion; they are more likely to sustain it until the system forces a reckoning. Their effectiveness makes them indispensable, their indispensability delays reform, and that delay ultimately necessitates the very disruption the system sought to prevent. Role Diffusion does not push high performers out through failure, but through clarity, as they recognize that staying would require accepting a version of the work that no longer tells the truth about its value or its cost.

Part II

When Informality Becomes Structure

Once Role Diffusion has taken hold, it does not remain a personal experience. It becomes a system condition. Informal arrangements that once seemed temporary begin to shape how work flows, how decisions are made, and how risk is managed. The system reorganizes itself quietly around what is available rather than what is accurate, and because outcomes continue to be met, the arrangement hardens into something that looks intentional.

Part II examines what happens after normalization gives way to dependence. It follows the arc from informal expansion to structural reliance, showing how systems come to depend on labor they have never formally acknowledged. What began as flexibility becomes necessity, and necessity resists correction. The work does not shrink back into its original boundaries; instead, it becomes embedded in routines, expectations, and assumptions that are difficult to unwind without disruption.

This section also explores why attempts at correction so often fail. Requests for redesign collide with outdated role descriptions. Escalation meets language designed to absorb rather than resolve. Formal systems arrive late, armed with documentation that no longer reflects reality, and treat consistency as fairness even when the work itself has changed. What feels like sudden conflict is revealed as the predictable outcome of prolonged avoidance.

Part II is where Role Diffusion shows its full shape. It reveals how outdated roles, selective modernization, and informal labor intersect to produce outcomes that feel unfair yet remain defensible on paper. It shows why capable people are kept in place while others move, why relief appears possible but unevenly applied, and why formal action often becomes inevitable only after informal correction has been quietly exhausted.

By the end of this section, the pattern is no longer ambiguous. What remains is not confusion about what is happening, but clarity about why it has been so difficult to interrupt. This is the point at which recognition becomes unavoidable, and where the work must either be realigned honestly or absorbed elsewhere. What follows from that clarity is the subject of what comes next.

CHAPTER 5

The Diagnostic Arc — From Normalization to Collision

How quiet accommodation hardens into inevitability

―――――――――◆◈◆―――――――――

Role Diffusion does not fail loudly. It succeeds quietly for a long time, which is why it is so often misunderstood when it finally breaks. By the time conflict appears, the system has already made a series of small decisions that rendered conflict unavoidable. Understanding this progression requires moving away from moments and toward mechanics, because the harm of Role Diffusion is cumulative, not episodic, and its endpoint is shaped long before anyone names it.

The arc begins with normalization, a phase that feels productive rather than problematic. Responsibilities expand incrementally, and each expansion appears justified by circumstance, urgency, or competence. Because nothing visibly collapses, the system reads continuity as confirmation. Work gets done, outcomes are met, and therefore no structural response feels necessary. However, normalization is not neutrality. It is a signal that informal arrangements have become dependable enough to replace formal ones, which is precisely what allows Role Diffusion to embed itself without resistance.

As normalization settles in, responsibility begins to detach from designation. The individual carries knowledge, oversight, and consequence that extend beyond their role, yet the role itself remains unchanged. This separation matters because authority follows designation, not practice, and therefore the individual is left managing outcomes they cannot formally shape. The system benefits from this arrangement because it concentrates accountability without redistributing power. Consequently, the longer normalization persists, the more expensive correction becomes, and the less incentive there is to pursue it.

What follows is dependency, although it is rarely named as such. The system begins to rely on the individual not simply for execution, but for stability. Questions route to them automatically. Decisions pause until they weigh in. Absence creates friction. At this stage, the individual is no longer just performing work; they are preventing failure. Yet because this dependency developed informally, it cannot be easily documented or addressed. The system depends on what it has not formally acknowledged, which means it cannot release the individual without exposing its own design gaps.

In the composite case, this dependency became visible when leadership hesitated to allow movement out of the role. The concern was not whether the individual was qualified for the next position, but whether anyone else could immediately absorb the responsibilities left behind. That hesitation revealed what normalization had already accomplished: the system had quietly reorganized itself around one person's capacity. However, because this reorganization had never been formalized, it could not be openly discussed without admitting that the role had long since exceeded its original scope.

In some cases, collision arrives earlier than expected, not through confrontation, but through quiet refusal. In the composite case referenced here, the individual requested a desk audit and job reclassification as a good-faith attempt to realign role and responsibility. The request was denied informally, accompanied by assurances that the process was unnecessary, unavailable, or best left untouched. What was not disclosed was that a formal, documented request would have required a written decision, one that could not have avoided either redesign or elevation. By discouraging documentation while denying relief, leadership effectively closed the last remaining informal avenue for correction, not resolving the imbalance but postponing its reckoning.

At this point in the arc, attempts at correction begin to surface, although they are often misread. The individual asks for clarity, redesign, or recognition that aligns with the work being done. These requests are framed not as demands, but as efforts to restore coherence between role and reality. Yet the system responds by referencing existing structures, pointing back to job descriptions, classifications, or clauses meant to justify flexibility. Therefore, the conversation stalls, not because the issue is unclear, but because acknowledging it would require change the system has already decided to postpone.

Collision emerges when informal labor meets formal scrutiny. This may take the form of grievance, audit, reclassification request, or legal process, but the form matters less than the function. The individual is no longer seeking accommodation; they are seeking reconciliation between what has been required and what has been recognized. The system, however, treats this moment as escalation rather than culmination. It evaluates the situation using documents that no longer describe the work, which allows it to argue consistency while ignoring substance.

In the case referenced here, the collision was sharpened by language that had previously seemed benign. The same clause used to justify flexibility during normalization was now invoked to deny misalignment under formal review. What had once allowed the system to avoid redesign was repurposed to defend that avoidance, effectively collapsing years of expanded responsibility into a single line of text. However, this move did not resolve the imbalance; it merely closed the door on informal correction, leaving formal action as the only remaining path.

What makes collision feel sudden to those outside it is that much of the strain was absorbed privately. High performers, in particular, tend to manage misalignment quietly, believing that continued excellence will eventually prompt recognition. Yet excellence delays correction when systems prioritize continuity over accuracy. Therefore, when the individual finally disengages, escalates, or exits, it appears abrupt, even though it followed a long period of deferred decision-making.

The diagnostic value of this arc lies in its predictability. Normalization leads to dependency. Dependency resists redesign. Resistance forces collision. Collision produces fallout, whether through exit, enforcement, or exhaustion. None of these stages are accidental, and none of them require malicious intent to unfold. They arise from incentives that reward short-term stability while deferring structural honesty, a trade-off that seems manageable until it no longer is.

Recognizing this arc earlier changes what is possible. It allows individuals to identify when normalization is hardening into dependency and to name the risk before correction becomes costly. It also allows systems to see that what feels like disruption at the point of collision is often the delayed result of choices made long before anyone raised their voice. Role Diffusion does not create conflict out of nowhere; it concentrates it, storing tension in informal arrangements until formal structures are forced to contend with what they have long ignored.

By the time collision occurs, the outcome is rarely satisfying for anyone involved. The individual leaves with clarity but little relief, while the system absorbs disruption it claimed to be avoiding. What is lost in that exchange is not simply talent, but the opportunity to intervene earlier, when responsibility could still be realigned with authority rather than defended through language. Understanding the diagnostic arc does not prevent Role Diffusion from occurring, but it does make its trajectory visible, and visibility is the first condition under which a system can choose something other than inevitability.

CHAPTER 6

The Role Diffusion Loop

Why relief becomes increasingly impossible over time

⟨⟨◇⟩⟩

By the time Role Diffusion becomes visible to the person carrying it, relief has already been structurally delayed. This is not because solutions were unavailable, but because the system quietly adapted to informal labor in ways that made correction feel optional rather than necessary. What initially appeared as flexibility hardened into dependence, and dependence reshaped incentives until relief was no longer aligned with institutional convenience. The result is a loop that sustains itself by converting accommodation into expectation and expectation into design, without ever admitting that design has occurred.

The loop begins when informal responsibility proves reliable. Tasks that were once absorbed as exceptions become integrated into daily operations, and because outcomes continue to be met, the system interprets continuity as success. However, this success is not neutral; it is underwritten by an individual absorbing complexity that the structure has declined to formalize. As long as performance remains high, the absence of visible failure suppresses urgency, and therefore the question of redesign never quite rises to the level of necessity.

As reliance deepens, relief becomes increasingly difficult to justify internally. Redesigning the role would require acknowledging that its scope has materially changed, which would trigger questions of classification, compensation, and equity. Redistributing the work would expose how much had been concentrated informally, creating short-term instability the system prefers to avoid. Therefore, leadership often reframes relief as impractical, even though it was the avoidance of early correction that made relief impractical in the first place.

At this stage, systems frequently substitute symbolic recognition for structural change. Praise, discretionary awards, or one-time payments are offered as evidence that the work has been noticed, even as the role itself remains untouched. These gestures are not meaningless, but they are misaligned. They acknowledge effort without correcting design, and therefore function less as reward than as containment. In some cases, such recognition also carries procedural consequences, limiting eligibility for other forms of advancement while documenting that leadership has already "responded." What is presented as appreciation becomes, in effect, a record of closure.

This substitution is particularly effective because it creates hope without commitment. The individual is led to believe, or even verbally told, that permanent correction is forthcoming, that the recognition offered now is a bridge rather than a substitute. As a result, they continue to carry the work in good faith, trusting that alignment will eventually follow. However, when these assurances are repeated without action, the pattern becomes clear: delay has replaced decision, and reassurance has replaced redesign. The loop tightens not through refusal, but through postponement.

Meanwhile, similarly situated colleagues advance. Their roles are formally reclassified, their pay adjusted, their scope acknowledged. The contrast is not subtle, and it reframes the situation entirely. What once felt like patience begins to feel like containment, because the system has demonstrated that it can act when it chooses to. The issue, then, is not feasibility but prioritization. Relief was never impossible; it was simply less convenient than continued reliance on undercompensated labor.

At this point, the individual's continued performance no longer protects the system from disruption; it enables avoidance. The loop depends on silence, documentation-free assurances, and symbolic gestures that signal responsiveness without requiring structural honesty. When the individual finally recognizes this, the nature of the relationship changes. What they sought was not reward, but truth. What they discover is that the system has been managing risk by distributing false reassurance rather than resolving misalignment.

Attempts to exit or transition often expose the loop most clearly. Movement is delayed because replacement is uncertain, yet replacement ultimately requires a level of compensation or authority that was previously deemed unnecessary. Vacancies linger. Responsibilities are re-evaluated only after departure. Filling the role at a higher level does not rewrite its history; it makes clear the avoidance that preceded it. The responsibilities were never misjudged—only carried informally for as long as the system could do so without confronting the implications of redesign.

Formal action enters the picture here not as escalation, but as consequence. The individual has exhausted informal avenues, accepted delay, and absorbed reassurance while continuing to perform. Once it becomes clear that structural correction is being indefinitely deferred, documentation becomes the only remaining mechanism capable of forcing a decision. The system may experience this as confrontation, yet it was the system's own reliance on ambiguity that made confrontation unavoidable.

What makes the Role Diffusion Loop so enduring is that it rarely appears malicious. Each step can be justified in isolation. Each delay can be explained. Each gesture can be defended. However, taken together, they form a coherent strategy of avoidance, one that preserves continuity by concentrating cost in a single place. Relief becomes impossible not because the work cannot be redesigned, but because redesign would expose choices the system has already made.

Naming this loop matters because it reframes what many capable people experience as personal disappointment into structural recognition. It explains why effort, excellence, and good faith are not sufficient to produce alignment once avoidance has been normalized. More importantly, it makes visible the point at which waiting no longer serves the individual, because the system has shown that delay is not a phase but a method. Without that visibility, the loop continues, quietly converting competence into compliance until departure becomes the only remaining form of honesty.

CHAPTER 7

When Formal Systems Meet Informal Labor
How documentation replaces reality once scrutiny begins

Formal systems are built to evaluate what can be seen, named, and documented. They rely on titles, classifications, written duties, and recorded decisions to determine whether work has been assigned fairly and whether outcomes align with policy. Informal labor, however, lives outside those boundaries. It accumulates through trust, necessity, and repetition, leaving little trace in the places formal systems are trained to look. When these two worlds collide, the result is rarely clarity. Instead, the collision exposes a mismatch between how work actually functions and how institutions are prepared to recognize it.

This mismatch explains why escalation often feels both necessary and futile. The individual arrives at a formal process carrying years of expanded responsibility that were never officially acknowledged, while the system responds by narrowing its focus to what is written rather than what was practiced. Therefore, the evaluation proceeds as though the role remained static, even though the labor required to sustain it did not. What feels like denial to the individual feels like procedural consistency to the institution, and the distance between those perspectives is where trust collapses.

The difficulty is not that formal systems are hostile to fairness, but that they are structurally ill-equipped to account for labor that was never formalized. Informal responsibility leaves no clean trail. It is rarely assigned in writing, rarely weighted in evaluation criteria, and rarely tied to authority or pay. As a result, when the individual attempts to reconcile lived experience with institutional review, the system defaults to the artifacts it recognizes. Job descriptions are treated as reality rather than reference points, and clauses intended for flexibility are elevated to definitive explanations.

It is within this gap that comparative concerns emerge. When individuals observe that relief, advancement, or redesign is available but selectively applied, the question shifts from workload to equity. Disparate outcomes demand interpretation, and when similarly situated colleagues receive promotions or reclassification while one person remains contained, patterns become visible that cannot be explained by performance alone. In the absence of any acknowledgment of informal labor, protected characteristics such as race become a reasonable lens through which to understand the disparity. This is not a leap; it is a rational response to observable difference.

Formal discrimination frameworks are designed to evaluate precisely this kind of differential treatment. They ask whether individuals performing similar work were treated differently and whether protected status plausibly explains the difference. However, when the work itself has been kept informal, the comparison becomes distorted. The system evaluates similarity based on written roles rather than functional reality, which allows it to argue that no disparity exists because, on paper, everyone was doing what their position required. In this way, the informality that enabled Role Diffusion also shields the system from scrutiny when inequity is challenged.

Language plays a decisive role at this point. Phrases such as *"other duties as assigned"*, once used to justify flexibility, are repurposed to neutralize comparison. Years of outcome-critical labor are collapsed into a single line of text, transforming sustained role substitution into incidental contribution. The system does not have to deny that work occurred; it simply reframes it as always having been part of the job. This move allows the institution to assert consistency while avoiding any examination of how responsibility was distributed or why relief flowed unevenly.

For the individual, this moment often feels like erasure rather than evaluation. The work they carried disappears into abstraction, while the formal system insists it has been accounted for. What is lost is not just recognition, but the ability to demonstrate inequity using the system's own criteria. The individual may experience this as discrimination being dismissed, when in fact it is informal labor being rendered invisible. However, the effect is the same. A claim rooted in lived disparity cannot survive in a framework that refuses to see how that disparity was produced.

This does not mean that bias is absent. It means that bias operates more effectively when structures allow it to remain implicit. Role Diffusion creates precisely those conditions. By keeping labor informal, systems retain discretion over when and for whom they will formalize relief. When that discretion is exercised unevenly, patterns of advantage and disadvantage emerge without ever being named as such. Formal processes then struggle to address the outcome because the mechanism that produced it was never officially acknowledged.

In the composite case we've been following, the collision between formal systems and informal labor made escalation unavoidable. Requests for redesign had been denied or deflected. Documentation had been discouraged. Assurance had replaced action. When relief was finally observed flowing elsewhere, the disparity could no longer be explained away as delay or constraint. Formal action followed not because the individual misunderstood the system, but because the system had exhausted every informal path to correction. What appeared as escalation was, in reality, a final attempt to force recognition of work that had long been relied upon but never named.

The tragedy of this collision is that it often satisfies no one. The individual leaves with clarity but little restoration, while the system maintains procedural innocence without addressing the design failure that produced the conflict. Informal labor remains unexamined, ready to be absorbed again by the next capable person. The formal process closes the case, but the mechanism persists, untouched.

Understanding what happens when formal systems meet informal labor reframes these outcomes. It reveals that many disputes labeled as performance issues, attitude problems, or unproven discrimination claims are better understood as structural failures of recognition. Role Diffusion does not negate the reality of bias; it explains how bias can persist without overt expression. It shows why inequity can be both experienced vividly by individuals and denied convincingly by institutions.

This recognition does not undo what has already occurred, but it clarifies what must be named earlier if repetition is to be avoided. Formal systems cannot correct what they are not designed to see. Until informal labor is acknowledged as a structural factor rather than an individual choice, collisions will continue to feel sudden and unresolved. Naming Role Diffusion does not guarantee justice, but it restores coherence to experiences that have long been dismissed as personal or inexplicable. And coherence, while not the same as relief, is the necessary ground from which more honest systems can eventually be built.

CHAPTER 8

When Work Outgrows Its Container
How outdated structures absorb modern complexity

————————⟨•❖•⟩————————

Work rarely stays still, even when organizations pretend that it does. Systems change, technology advances, expectations compound, and risk migrates in ways that make yesterday's job descriptions increasingly inadequate. Yet many organizations continue to treat roles as fixed artifacts, as though what was sufficient at one moment in time should remain sufficient indefinitely. This refusal to acknowledge evolution is not benign. It creates the conditions under which Role Diffusion accelerates, because when work changes faster than roles are updated, the excess does not disappear. It settles somewhere, usually on the shoulders of the person most capable of carrying it.

The mismatch begins quietly. New tools are introduced. Processes become more automated, more interconnected, and more exposed to error. What once required routine execution now demands judgment, technical fluency, and the ability to anticipate downstream consequences. However, instead of redesigning roles to reflect these new demands, organizations often layer the work onto existing positions, assuming that adaptation will occur organically. The role remains described in language that reflects a previous era, while the work itself evolves in complexity and consequence. This gap becomes fertile ground for Role Diffusion, because it allows systems to extract higher-level labor without formally acknowledging that the work now requires higher-level skill.

What makes this particularly corrosive is that evolution is not evenly distributed. Some roles are modernized quickly, either because failure would be visible or because no individual is available to quietly absorb the change. In those cases, organizations invest. They hire contractors, reclassify positions, or create entirely new roles to meet the demands of the work as it actually exists. Elsewhere, however, evolution is ignored precisely because someone has already stepped into the gap. When a capable individual adapts successfully, their adaptation becomes the justification for inaction. The system concludes that redesign is unnecessary, not because the work has not changed, but because the change has been privately managed.

This selective modernization reveals something important about how organizations allocate resources. Modernization is treated not as a response to evolving work, but as a response to visible strain. Where strain is hidden by individual effort, the system feels no urgency to act. Where strain cannot be concealed, investment suddenly becomes possible. The result is an uneven landscape in which some people receive structural support while others are left to compensate alone, even when the technical demands placed upon them are equal or greater. The system appears consistent because it responds to pressure, but the pressure itself has been distributed unevenly.

For those carrying evolved work inside stagnant roles, attempts to name the mismatch are often reframed. Requests for reclassification or redesign are interpreted as ambition rather than diagnosis, as though noticing misalignment were equivalent to seeking personal advancement. This reframing is convenient because it shifts the focus away from the system's failure to update its own structures and places it instead on the individual's motives. The work remains described as unchanged, and therefore any challenge to that description can be dismissed as subjective or self-interested. In this way, outdated roles become tools of invalidation, not because they accurately reflect reality, but because they provide cover for avoiding it.

Technology intensifies this dynamic. As systems grow more complex, the cost of error rises, and the value of foresight increases. Individuals who possess advanced technical skills, pattern recognition, or cross-functional understanding become essential to preventing failure. Yet when those skills are not listed as requirements, they are treated as bonuses rather than necessities. The organization benefits from their application while maintaining the fiction that the role itself remains simple. This fiction allows compensation and classification to lag far behind the actual demands of the work, effectively converting specialized expertise into unpaid infrastructure.

Selective relief further sharpens the imbalance. When organizations eventually act, they often do so around the individual who has been raising concerns rather than for them. Contractors are brought in to support others. New positions are created to accommodate colleagues. Reclassifications occur elsewhere, sometimes after the individual has already articulated the need for modernization. These moves demonstrate that the system understands the problem well enough to solve it, but chooses where and when to do so. For the person who has been absorbing the work all along, this sequence feels less like coincidence and more like confirmation. Relief was never impossible. It was simply deferred until it could be applied without addressing the original misalignment.

This is the point at which perceptions of unfairness harden into recognition. When similarly situated colleagues receive investment while one person remains contained, the question is no longer whether roles need to evolve, but why evolution is being applied selectively. In such conditions, protected characteristics such as race become salient not because they are introduced opportunistically, but because they align with observable patterns of who receives relief and who does not. The system's insistence that roles have not changed becomes increasingly difficult to reconcile with the evidence of change everywhere else.

What makes this especially difficult to challenge is that outdated roles provide a defensible paper trail. Formal systems rely on descriptions that no longer capture reality and then use those descriptions to evaluate fairness. The evolved work disappears into informality, while the role remains frozen in time. When grievances are raised, the system points to the description as proof that nothing exceptional has occurred. In this way, role stagnation does more than enable Role Diffusion; it protects it from scrutiny.

Gradually, a pattern becomes unmistakable. The system advances by modernizing selectively, correcting itself only where it can no longer rely on quiet accommodation. Those who adapt most successfully are left to subsidize delay, praised for their flexibility while constrained by structures that refuse to evolve alongside the work. When they eventually disengage, escalate, or leave, the system often moves quickly to formalize what it had long denied, confirming after the fact that the work had indeed outgrown its original design.

For the reader, the recognition here is not abstract. If the work you are doing requires skills, judgment, and technical fluency that are absent from your role description, the issue is not your ambition or impatience. It is that the system has stopped telling the truth about the work it relies on. Role Diffusion thrives in that silence, because silence allows evolution to be managed privately rather than acknowledged structurally. Once this dynamic is visible, the question shifts from whether you are asking for too much to whether the role has been allowed to fall too far behind the work it demands. That clarity is what makes the next question unavoidable: if this mechanism holds here, how does it show up elsewhere?

CHAPTER 9

The Pressure Test

How Role Diffusion adapts across systems

Once Role Diffusion is clearly named, its presence becomes difficult to confine to a single workplace or sector. The pattern is not industry-specific; it is system-responsive. Wherever work evolves faster than roles are updated, wherever informality is rewarded more quickly than redesign, and wherever continuity is valued over accuracy, Role Diffusion adapts and persists. The surface language changes, the justifications shift, but the underlying logic remains intact, which is precisely what makes the concept durable rather than anecdotal.

In government environments, Role Diffusion thrives inside classification rigidity and risk aversion. Roles are anchored to formal descriptions that move slowly, often requiring lengthy review processes to update, while policy, technology, and compliance demands accelerate. When new systems are introduced or regulations shift, the additional labor does not wait for reclassification. It is absorbed informally by those who can navigate complexity without triggering visible failure. Because stability is prized, adaptability becomes a private burden rather than a structural priority. Incrementally, responsibility migrates upward in practice while authority remains fixed on paper, and formal processes later rely on those same outdated descriptions to argue that nothing exceptional occurred.

In healthcare settings, the mechanism is driven by urgency and moral pressure. The work expands because lives, outcomes, and safety are at stake, and therefore refusal feels ethically untenable. Clinicians and administrators alike absorb additional responsibilities because delay carries immediate human cost. However, the normalization of crisis labor makes Role Diffusion difficult to detect. What begins as stepping in during extraordinary circumstances becomes routine expectation, and because care continues to be delivered, the system interprets sacrifice as sustainability. Relief is delayed until burnout or attrition forces recognition, at which point the system responds reactively rather than redesigning proactively.

Education presents a different adaptation, shaped by mission and emotional labor. Teachers, counselors, and administrators routinely absorb responsibilities beyond instruction, responding to social, technological, and behavioral demands that far exceed the scope of traditional roles. These expansions are framed as dedication rather than structural change, which allows systems to benefit from unpaid labor while preserving the fiction that the role itself remains unchanged. Because the work is relational and outcomes are diffuse, the burden is often individualized, making Role Diffusion appear as personal overwhelm rather than institutional design failure.

In nonprofit organizations, Role Diffusion is frequently justified through scarcity narratives. Limited funding and staffing are treated as permanent conditions, and adaptability is framed as virtue rather than necessity. Individuals take on expanded responsibilities out of commitment to the mission, trusting that sacrifice is both expected and temporary. However, scarcity becomes a convenient rationale for avoiding redesign, even when funding grows or organizational complexity increases. The system relies on goodwill to absorb evolved work, while formal roles remain static to protect budgets and optics.

Technology-driven environments introduce yet another variation. Speed is valorized, ownership is emphasized, and formal boundaries are often dismissed as obstacles to innovation. Responsibility expands rapidly because the work demands it, but authority does not always follow. Individuals are encouraged to "own" outcomes without being granted the decision-making power or compensation that ownership implies. Because agility is celebrated, Role Diffusion is reframed as opportunity, and questioning scope is sometimes interpreted as resistance rather than diagnosis. In the long arc, the absence of formal alignment creates instability that is later addressed through restructuring, often after key contributors have already exited.

Across these systems, the differences are instructive but secondary. The same sequence unfolds repeatedly. Work evolves. Roles lag. Capable individuals absorb the gap. Informal arrangements normalize. Dependency forms. Relief is delayed. Formal systems later intervene using artifacts that no longer describe reality. The justifications vary, but the outcome does not. Role Diffusion survives because it adapts to the language and values of each environment while preserving its core function: allowing systems to extract evolved labor without paying the cost of redesign.

What this pressure test reveals is not that some industries are worse than others, but that Role Diffusion is most powerful where incentives reward short-term continuity over long-term accuracy. In each setting, the system benefits from adaptability while externalizing the cost onto individuals. Those costs remain invisible until the individual can no longer carry them quietly, at which point the system experiences the disruption it claimed to be avoiding.

This recognition widens the lens, because when the pattern feels familiar across contexts, it is structural rather than situational. The problem is not that one organization failed to manage workload, or that one leader made a poor decision. It is that many systems are designed to respond to strain only after it becomes visible, and Role Diffusion specializes in keeping strain hidden by concentrating it in people who can endure it longest.

The pressure test does not prove that Role Diffusion exists; it demonstrates that it travels. It shows that the concept holds under varied constraints, cultures, and missions, which is the mark of a framework rather than a complaint. Once seen, it becomes difficult to dismiss as personal misfortune or sector-specific dysfunction. What remains is the recognition that wherever work evolves and roles do not, Role Diffusion will find a way to settle, adapt, and persist.

And it is here, after the mechanism has been seen operating across systems, that the next question can be approached with clarity rather than confusion: not whether the pattern is real, but what choices remain once it has been recognized.

Part III

After Recognition

Recognition changes the terrain. Once Role Diffusion is named clearly, it can no longer be mistaken for overwork, ambition, impatience, or poor boundary-setting. What previously felt confusing becomes legible, and what once seemed personal reveals itself as patterned. However, recognition does not immediately resolve anything. In fact, it often sharpens tension, because clarity arrives before relief, and awareness precedes action.

This is the point at which many capable people feel stranded. They can no longer pretend the misalignment is temporary, yet they remain embedded in structures that depend on their continued accommodation. The work still matters. The mission may still resonate. The relationships may still feel real. And yet the role, as defined, no longer tells the truth about what is being carried. Recognition does not dissolve these attachments; it complicates them.

What follows recognition is not collapse, but calculation. Individuals begin to assess what staying actually costs, not just in hours or energy, but in coherence. They weigh the possibility of redesign against the evidence of repeated deferral. They consider escalation while remembering how informality has been used to neutralize previous attempts at correction. They notice how language has been deployed to reframe diagnosis as ambition, and how delay has been justified as patience. The system, meanwhile, continues to reward continuity, often mistaking endurance for consent.

Part III begins here, in this unsettled space between seeing and leaving. The chapters that follow do not offer prescriptions or moral conclusions. Instead, they examine the decision points that emerge once Role Diffusion can no longer be unseen. They explore why fairness, rather than fatigue, becomes the threshold that determines movement. They name the moments when staying begins to require self-erasure, and when leaving becomes less an act of defiance than an act of alignment.

This section also addresses the quiet grief that accompanies clarity. There is loss in recognizing that effort was not misunderstood but strategically absorbed. There is loss in seeing that correction was possible but selectively applied. And there is loss in accepting that systems often change only after departure, formal action, or exposure forces their hand. These losses do not make departure dramatic, but they make it final.

Part III does not frame exit as failure or escalation as aggression. It treats both as outcomes that emerge when informal labor has been relied upon long enough to distort choice. The focus here is not on what should have happened, but on what becomes possible once denial is no longer an option. Clarity does not guarantee justice, but it restores agency, and agency is the condition under which decisions can be made without shame.

From this point forward, the work turns toward consequence. Not in the sense of punishment or resolution, but in the sense of reckoning with what recognition demands. When Role Diffusion is no longer invisible, something must change. The only remaining question is where that change will be absorbed—by the individual, or by the system that relied on their silence.

<hr>

CHAPTER 10

The Fairness Threshold
When staying becomes morally incoherent

People rarely leave roles the moment work becomes heavy. Difficulty alone is not what drives capable people away, nor is complexity, pace, or responsibility. Many remain engaged long after their roles have stretched beyond their original boundaries, absorbing expansion because the work feels meaningful and the effort feels temporary. What eventually changes is not stamina, but perception. There comes a moment when the imbalance stops feeling situational and begins to feel unjust, and that moment marks the crossing of a threshold that cannot be reversed.

The fairness threshold is reached when effort and recognition diverge in ways that can no longer be explained by timing or circumstance. Early on, expanded responsibility may feel like an investment, a period of proving oneself while structures catch up. However, when that catching up never arrives, and when assurances are repeated without material change, the individual begins to notice patterns rather than promises. The work continues to grow, yet the role remains static, and the explanation offered for this stasis shifts from temporary delay to quiet normalization.

What distinguishes this threshold from ordinary frustration is comparison. The individual observes not only their own stalled alignment, but the movement occurring around them. Others receive redesign, relief, or elevation, sometimes for narrower scopes of work, sometimes after less time, sometimes through newly created paths that did not exist when similar requests were made earlier. At this point, the system's capacity to act is no longer in question. What comes into focus instead is selectivity, and selectivity reframes the experience entirely.

Once selectivity is visible, patience begins to feel like consent. The individual recognizes that continued accommodation is not buying time toward correction, but underwriting a structure that has chosen to rely on them as they are. The work no longer feels like growth because it does not lead anywhere. It feels like containment, a holding pattern that benefits the system while asking the individual to suspend their own coherence. This is the moment when endurance stops being virtuous and starts being costly.

The fairness threshold is also crossed when language begins to obscure rather than clarify. Praise is offered without change. One-time gestures replace durable alignment. Requests for redesign are reframed as ambition, and diagnosis is recast as impatience. The system insists that nothing has changed while simultaneously adjusting around the individual in ways that contradict that claim. When words no longer match outcomes, trust erodes, not because of disappointment, but because of inconsistency.

At this stage, the individual often realizes that the issue is no longer about whether they can continue, but whether continuing requires self-erasure. Remaining in the role means accepting that their labor will be treated as elastic and their clarity as inconvenient. It means watching correction arrive elsewhere while being told, implicitly or explicitly, that their situation is different without being told why. Fairness does not demand identical outcomes, but it does require intelligible ones, and once intelligibility disappears, so does justification.

The fairness threshold is personal, but it is not arbitrary. It emerges from accumulated evidence, from watching how the system responds when pressed and whom it chooses to accommodate. It is reached when the individual understands that the misalignment is not an oversight, but a condition that has been managed deliberately through delay, deflection, and selective action. At that point, staying becomes an active choice to accept inequity rather than a passive hope for resolution.

Crossing this threshold does not immediately produce action. Often it produces stillness, a quiet recalibration in which the individual stops volunteering flexibility and begins observing consequences. They may continue to perform, but the internal contract has shifted. The belief that effort will eventually be met with fairness has been replaced by the recognition that fairness is not forthcoming under current conditions. This recognition changes how every subsequent interaction is interpreted, because promises are now weighed against patterns rather than intent.

What makes the fairness threshold decisive is that it cannot be unseen. Once crossed, returning to earlier explanations feels dishonest. The individual can no longer tell themselves that misalignment is temporary or that silence is strategic. They see clearly that remaining requires absorbing the cost of inequity indefinitely, while leaving, escalating, or forcing documentation redistributes that cost back toward the system. The choice becomes less about preference and more about integrity.

The fairness threshold does not announce itself dramatically. It arrives quietly, often after the system has already benefited from years of unacknowledged labor. When it is reached, the outcome is not impulsive departure or sudden confrontation, but inevitability. Whatever follows—redesign, escalation, or exit—flows from the same recognition: that fairness delayed long enough becomes fairness denied, and once that truth is understood, staying no longer feels neutral.

CHAPTER 11

What Organizations Could Do
(But Consistently Avoid)

Why systems delay correction until disruption is unavoidable

Most organizations are not incapable of addressing Role Diffusion. They are simply disinclined to do so early, when correction would require humility rather than disruption. By the time action feels unavoidable, the costs have shifted, and the system is no longer deciding whether to change, but how much fallout it can tolerate. This is not a failure of knowledge. It is a failure of timing, compounded by incentives that reward short-term continuity over long-term coherence.

Early intervention would begin with accuracy. Roles would be treated as living structures rather than archival documents, updated to reflect not only what is assigned, but what is required. This would mean acknowledging that work evolves unevenly and that technological change, policy expansion, and risk exposure alter the nature of responsibility long before job descriptions are revised. However, accuracy introduces obligation. Once a role is described honestly, the system must contend with what that description implies about authority, compensation, and equity, and those implications are often more disruptive than silence.

Another point of intervention lies in documentation. Organizations could insist that sustained expansions of responsibility be recorded formally rather than absorbed informally. Doing so would surface misalignment earlier, before normalization hardens into dependence. Yet documentation removes deniability. It creates records that require response, timelines that demand decision, and visibility that complicates selective action. As a result, systems often tolerate ambiguity because ambiguity preserves flexibility, even as it erodes fairness.

An even earlier intervention lies in acknowledgement. Before redesign, before reclassification, before documentation is formalized, organizations could speak honestly about what is already occurring. This would mean naming, on the record, that a role has expanded beyond its original scope, that responsibility has shifted in practice, and that the system is relying on work it has not formally reconciled. Such conversations do not require immediate resolution, but they do require truth.

The refusal to acknowledge observable change is not neutral. When leaders dismiss concerns as complaining, frame diagnosis as personal dissatisfaction, or insist that nothing has changed despite mounting evidence, they force individuals to question their own perception of reality. This erodes trust more quickly than delay alone. It communicates that accuracy is less important than maintaining the appearance of continuity, and that raising concerns threatens stability rather than protecting it.

Honest acknowledgement, even without immediate correction, preserves dignity. It signals that the system can see what the individual sees, even if it is not yet prepared to act. When acknowledgement is withheld, the burden shifts entirely onto the individual to either endure quietly or escalate forcefully, transforming what could have been a collaborative reckoning into an adversarial one.

Organizations could also separate adaptability from exploitation by clarifying the difference between temporary stretch and permanent substitution. Flexibility has value when it is bounded, time-limited, and reciprocated. Without those constraints, flexibility becomes a one-way transfer of burden. Drawing that distinction would require leaders to notice when the same individual is repeatedly absorbing complexity and to ask whether the role itself has changed. This kind of noticing is possible, but it requires attention to patterns rather than outcomes, and many systems are optimized to measure results without examining how they are achieved.

Modernization is another available, but underused, lever. Organizations routinely update tools, platforms, and processes while leaving the human structures around them unchanged. This creates a mismatch in which sophisticated work is expected to be performed inside outdated roles. Addressing this would mean aligning role design with actual skill requirements and acknowledging when evolved work demands elevated judgment or technical fluency. However, modernization exposes cost. It reveals where systems have relied on unpaid complexity, and correcting that reliance requires investment that may not have been budgeted or planned for.

Leadership behavior plays a decisive role here. Leaders could respond to early signals of misalignment by treating them as diagnostic rather than aspirational. Instead of framing requests for redesign as ambition or impatience, they could interpret them as indicators that the system's structures are lagging behind reality. Doing so would shift the burden of proof away from individuals and toward the role itself. Yet this shift challenges deeply held norms about loyalty, patience, and endurance, especially in environments that equate quiet accommodation with professionalism.

Perhaps most importantly, organizations could establish thresholds beyond which informality is no longer acceptable. Informal labor is often justified as efficient, but efficiency without boundaries invites distortion. Clear thresholds would signal when sustained responsibility must be formalized, redistributed, or compensated, rather than indefinitely absorbed.

Importantly, such thresholds are not speculative. In many institutional contexts, particularly within regulated systems, formal guidance already exists that defines when work has become significant enough to require documentation, redesign, or reclassification. Sustained duties that occupy a meaningful portion of an individual's time—especially when they require higher-level judgment or skill—are widely recognized as no longer incidental. At that point, continuing to rely on catch-all language or informal flexibility is not an oversight; it is a decision to avoid the implications of accuracy.

The persistent absence of enforcement is therefore not a lack of standards, but a lack of will. Systems benefit from elasticity when thresholds remain unacknowledged, because elasticity allows responsibility to expand without triggering the obligations that formal recognition would impose. In this way, Role Diffusion is not enabled by the absence of rules, but by the selective disregard of ones that already exist.

What prevents these interventions from becoming common practice is not ignorance, but incentive alignment. Systems are rewarded for stability, not for accuracy, and disruption is penalized even when it leads to healthier structures. Leaders are often evaluated on continuity rather than coherence, and therefore learn to manage misalignment quietly rather than confront it openly. By degrees, this produces organizations that appear functional while relying heavily on invisible labor to remain so.

When organizations do act, they often do so late and selectively. Roles are updated after departure, resources are allocated after escalation, and corrections are made once exposure becomes unavoidable. These actions confirm that intervention was always possible, but not prioritized. The lesson internalized by those who carried the work is not that they asked too much, but that they asked at the wrong time, in a system that only responds once the cost of inaction exceeds the cost of change.

This chapter does not argue that organizations are incapable of fairness, but that fairness requires intentional friction. It requires slowing down long enough to notice where work has outgrown its containers and being willing to absorb discomfort early rather than fallout later. Without that willingness, Role Diffusion remains a rational strategy for preserving continuity, even as it undermines trust, equity, and retention.

What organizations could do has always been clear. What they rarely do is choose accuracy over convenience before accuracy is forced upon them. And in that gap between capability and choice, Role Diffusion continues to thrive, not because it is invisible, but because it is allowed.

CHAPTER 12

Language That Protects People Earlier

Why early interruption so often fails, even when danger is sensed

━━━━━━━━━━━◆❖◆━━━━━━━━━

Language does not merely describe work; it shapes what can be acknowledged, challenged, and corrected. In organizations, the words used to frame responsibility determine whether expansion is recognized as evolution or dismissed as accommodation. When language lags behind reality, it creates a vacuum in which Role Diffusion thrives, not because anyone intends harm, but because the system lacks the vocabulary to interrupt what it quietly depends on.

Early protection begins with naming sustained responsibility as such. Temporary stretch and permanent substitution are often spoken about interchangeably, yet they function very differently. When language treats ongoing responsibility as incidental, it allows the system to avoid deciding whether the role itself has changed. Precision matters here, because without it, individuals are left negotiating misalignment using terms that minimize what they are carrying. The absence of accurate language does not neutralize the work; it renders it invisible.

Documentation is one of the earliest points at which language can intervene. When expanded responsibilities remain undocumented, they exist only as expectation, which makes them difficult to contest later. However, documentation is often discouraged under the guise of efficiency or trust, as though writing things down signals mistrust rather than clarity. This discouragement protects the system by preserving ambiguity, even as it exposes individuals to prolonged imbalance. Language that protects earlier insists on record not as accusation, but as alignment, creating a shared reference point before normalization hardens into dependence.

The way requests are framed also matters. When individuals are forced to speak about misalignment using the language of ambition, their diagnosis is easily dismissed as self-interest. Requests for redesign are recast as promotion-seeking, and structural concerns are reframed as personal dissatisfaction. Protective language resists this collapse by anchoring requests in function rather than aspiration. It describes what the work requires, what decisions are being made informally, and what risks are being managed without authority. By doing so, it shifts the conversation from desire to design.

Equally important is how organizations respond. Language that deflects by praising effort without addressing structure signals closure rather than care. One-time acknowledgments, discretionary awards, and verbal assurances create the appearance of responsiveness while leaving the underlying misalignment intact. When such gestures are treated as resolution, they foreclose further conversation by implying that the issue has been addressed. Protective language, by contrast, keeps questions open until structure aligns with reality.

Timing amplifies the impact of language. Words offered early can prevent escalation by forcing clarity while adjustment is still feasible. The same words offered late often sound defensive, even when they are accurate. This is why language that protects people earlier must be used before fairness is breached, not after. Once selectivity becomes visible, trust in language erodes, and even sincere explanations are filtered through accumulated evidence of delay.

The role of leadership is decisive here. Leaders who use language to surface misalignment rather than smooth it over create conditions for early correction. This requires tolerating discomfort, because naming misalignment often reveals inconvenient truths about workload, classification, and resourcing. However, discomfort absorbed early prevents harm later. Language that protects does not promise resolution; it commits to recognition, which is the necessary first step toward redesign.

When language fails to protect early, individuals are left with few options. Silence becomes complicity. Accommodation becomes expectation. Eventually, documentation becomes defensive rather than corrective, introduced only after informal avenues have closed. At that point, language can still force acknowledgment, but it does so through confrontation rather than collaboration. The system experiences this as escalation, even though escalation is simply what remains once earlier opportunities for clarity have been exhausted.

This is why language matters long before conflict arises. It determines whether Role Diffusion is interrupted while it is still reversible or allowed to harden into a condition that requires formal action to unwind. Language that protects people earlier does not eliminate the need for courage or judgment, but it changes the terrain on which those qualities are exercised. It gives shape to work that would otherwise disappear into expectation and provides a means of naming misalignment before fairness is breached.

When accurate language is absent, Role Diffusion proceeds quietly, sustained by silence and softened by praise. When accurate language is present, it introduces friction that systems may resist but cannot easily ignore. That friction is not obstruction; it is information. And information, when acknowledged early enough, remains one of the few tools capable of preventing clarity from arriving only after cost has already been paid.

CHAPTER THIRTEEN

Leaving Without Shame

What becomes possible once recognition is irreversible

Leaving is often described as a decision, but for those who have lived inside Role Diffusion, it rarely feels that simple. It arrives after a long period of recognition, one in which clarity accumulates faster than options. By the time departure becomes visible, the internal work has already been done. The individual has measured effort against outcome, patience against pattern, and hope against evidence, and the conclusion has emerged gradually rather than dramatically. Leaving, in this sense, is not a rupture. It is the final alignment of what was already understood.

Shame enters this moment quietly, usually disguised as self-questioning. It asks why endurance was offered for so long, why documentation came late, why trust was extended when it should have been withheld. These questions feel responsible, even ethical, yet they rest on an assumption that the individual failed to act when action was possible. What they overlook is that action requires legibility, and legibility depends on language. Without language that could be heard, early resistance would not have produced correction. It would have produced dismissal, reframing, or isolation, all while the work continued unchanged.

Understanding this alters the meaning of departure. Leaving is not an admission that something could not be handled. It is an acknowledgment that what was being handled no longer had a truthful container. The role had stopped reflecting the work, the system had stopped responding to diagnosis, and fairness had crossed a threshold from delay into denial. Staying beyond that point would have required erasing what had already been recognized, and recognition cannot be undone without cost.

There is often grief here, not only for the work itself, but for the version of the system that was hoped for. Many people remain longer than they should because they believe that clarity will eventually be met with care, that persistence will be rewarded with redesign, or that fairness will assert itself if given enough time. Letting go of that belief is not cynicism. It is the acceptance that systems do not change simply because the right person endures long enough. They change when structures are forced to reconcile with reality.

Leaving without shame also means releasing responsibility for outcomes that were never formally entrusted. Role Diffusion blurs ownership so thoroughly that individuals begin to feel accountable for what happens after they go, even when authority never accompanied responsibility. This sense of lingering obligation is a residue of informal labor, not a measure of loyalty. Once the individual is no longer positioned to shape outcomes honestly, continuing to carry that weight serves no one, least of all the system that relied on their silence.

Some departures are quiet. Others involve escalation, documentation, or formal action. The form matters less than the function. In each case, leaving redistributes cost back toward the structure that avoided absorbing it earlier. This redistribution is often framed as disruption, yet it is more accurately understood as delayed correction. What feels abrupt to the system is the consequence of choices made over time, choices that relied on one person's willingness to hold more than their role acknowledged.

The temptation to reinterpret the past is strong at this stage. People may feel pressure to frame their departure as growth, opportunity, or personal evolution, as though naming misalignment directly would be impolite or excessive. While these narratives can be useful externally, they are not required internally. Leaving without shame does not demand that the experience be softened to preserve comfort. It only requires that it be understood accurately, without assigning fault where structure was the determining force.

Clarity does not erase harm, but it does prevent it from being internalized. When individuals understand that they were operating inside a system that rewarded accommodation and resisted correction, they can stop treating endurance as evidence of complicity. They can see that what they offered was competence, good faith, and restraint, and that these qualities were used longer than they should have been because the system found them convenient. That recognition restores dignity without requiring vindication.

This book has not argued that leaving is always the right choice. It has argued that staying becomes untenable once recognition arrives and fairness is breached without remedy. At that point, leaving is not a failure of commitment, but a refusal to continue carrying what the system has declined to hold. Shame dissolves when responsibility is returned to its proper place.

What remains after leaving is not emptiness, but coherence. The individual carries forward the knowledge that their experience was real, patterned, and intelligible, even when it was not acknowledged in the moment. They no longer need the system to validate what they have already understood.

The work they did mattered, even if it was never named correctly. And the decision to stop offering silent accommodation becomes, finally, an act of alignment rather than escape.

Leaving without shame is not about reclaiming power or proving a point. It is about choosing to live inside a version of work that tells the truth. Once that truth is known, there is no obligation to stay where it must be denied.

CONCLUSION

What Remains When the Pattern Is Named

Why clarity resolves conflict without rewriting the past

———————————⟨❖⟩———————————

Role Diffusion persists for as long as it remains unnamed. Once named, it does not disappear, but it does lose its ability to disguise itself as personal weakness, poor attitude, or failure to cope. What remains after the pattern is recognized is not certainty, but coherence. Events that once felt isolated align into sequence. Decisions that once felt impulsive reveal themselves as cumulative. And departures that were questioned, criticized, or misunderstood settle into their proper context as outcomes rather than reactions.

For many, the most difficult part of this clarity is not what it reveals about work, but what it exposes about proximity. When someone leaves a role shaped by Role Diffusion, the decision rarely affects them alone. It reaches into households, partnerships, and shared plans, where the logic of endurance is often mistaken for stability. From the outside, the job may look successful, the compensation sufficient, the recognition real. What cannot be seen easily is the cost of sustaining that appearance, or the way harm migrates when systems rely on one person to absorb what they refuse to correct.

This is where misunderstanding often hardens. When the mechanism remains invisible, departure is interpreted as choice rather than consequence. The person leaving is told they are not being a team player, that everyone has hard jobs, that patience would eventually pay off. These responses are not cruelty; they are the natural conclusions drawn when only outcomes are visible and structure is not. Without language for Role Diffusion, even those closest to the situation may mistake clarity for instability and coherence for risk.

Naming the pattern changes that dynamic. It allows departure to be understood not as withdrawal, but as the final refusal to continue subsidizing a system that has already declined to change. It reframes leaving as an act of alignment rather than abandonment, and it restores proportion to conversations that had become moralized by misunderstanding. The decision is no longer about resilience or loyalty, but about the point at which fairness was breached and repair was refused.

What this book ultimately leaves behind is not instruction, but permission. Permission to stop rewriting the past in search of a version where endurance would have been rewarded. Permission to release the belief that waiting longer would have produced a different outcome. Permission to let go of the idea that clarity arrived too late, when in fact it arrived exactly when it could no longer be ignored. Role Diffusion does not end because someone tries harder. It ends because someone stops agreeing to carry what has never been theirs to hold alone.

There is also a quieter permission embedded here, one that extends beyond the individual who leaves. It allows partners, families, and colleagues to understand that stability built on unacknowledged labor is fragile, even when it looks secure. It invites those who benefit indirectly from that stability to see the cost they did not have to pay, and to recognize why asking someone to stay can sometimes mean asking them to disappear.

Nothing in this book promises that leaving will be easy, or that clarity will be met with affirmation. Systems rarely thank those who expose their limits. Relationships may need time to recalibrate. Financial and emotional uncertainty may follow. And yet, what replaces Role Diffusion is not chaos. It is integrity. The work that follows may still be demanding, but it will no longer require silence to sustain it.

What remains, finally, is truth. The truth that work evolved while roles stood still. The truth that capability was rewarded with containment. The truth that fairness delayed became fairness denied. And the truth that leaving was not a failure to endure, but a refusal to continue absorbing what should have been carried by design.

Once that truth is known, it does not ask to be acted upon immediately. It simply stands, steady and unmovable, waiting for the moment when alignment matters more than appearance. When that moment arrives, the path forward is no longer a question of courage, but of coherence. And coherence, once chosen, does not require justification.

APPENDIX

Conceptual Neighbors (Not Sources)

Where Role Diffusion sits among related ideas without being replaced by them

———————————————<<<>>>———————————————

The concept of Role Diffusion exists alongside, but is distinct from, several bodies of thought that address work, labor, and organizational behavior. These frameworks illuminate related experiences, yet none sufficiently account for the specific mechanism described in this book, which is why Role Diffusion required independent naming.

Discussions of **burnout** focus primarily on exhaustion as an outcome, often emphasizing emotional depletion, workload, or insufficient recovery. While burnout may result from Role Diffusion, it does not explain how responsibility migrates structurally without recognition, nor why capable individuals remain engaged long after misalignment has become evident.

The idea of **role creep** acknowledges that job responsibilities can expand gradually, yet it typically treats this expansion as incidental or manageable rather than as a system-level dependency. Role Diffusion differs in that it describes not just expansion, but normalization, reliance, and later defense of that expansion through formal mechanisms.

Frameworks centered on **organizational justice** and **equity** address fairness in outcomes and treatment, particularly across protected classes. While these perspectives are essential, they often evaluate disparity after it has surfaced rather than explaining how informal labor arrangements harden into defensible inequity before formal comparison occurs. Role Diffusion clarifies how inequity can be produced quietly through role stagnation long before it is litigated or acknowledged.

Concepts related to **informal work** and **emotional labor** recognize labor that falls outside formal recognition, especially in caregiving or relational roles. Role Diffusion intersects with these ideas but extends beyond them by focusing on decision-making authority, technical responsibility, and risk management that migrate without corresponding structural alignment.

Finally, leadership and management literature often emphasizes **adaptability**, **ownership**, and **initiative** as virtues. Role Diffusion reveals how these qualities, when unbounded and unreconciled with role design, become mechanisms through which systems avoid redesign while continuing to benefit from evolved labor.

These conceptual neighbors help contextualize the terrain in which Role Diffusion operates, but they do not replace it. Role Diffusion names a specific, repeatable process that explains why capable individuals become indispensable without becoming eligible for relief, and why departure often becomes the only remaining path once recognition arrives too late to preserve alignment.

www.ingramcontent.com/pod-product-compliance
Lightning Source LLC
Chambersburg PA
CBHW050644190326
41458CB00008B/2416